629.22

629.22

Young, Robert

MINIATURE VEHICLES

DEMCO

MINIATURE VEHICLES

MINIATURE VEHICLES

By Robert Young

DILLON PRESS
New York

Maxwell Macmillan Canada
Toronto

Maxwell Macmillan International
New York   Oxford   Singapore   Sydney

For Joyce,
who helps make writing worth reading

Acknowledgments
With many thanks to the following people for their generous help: Dave Bell, Donna Braden, Diane Cardinale, Paul Carr, Phil Christensen, Judy Ellis, Dave Horton, Avi Jerchower, Chris JeRue, Eric Lanz, Ted Lannom, Charlie Mack, Everett Marshall, Lisa McKendall, Joann McLaughlin, Mike Meyer, Joe O'Brien, Beatrice Parsons, Dave Reina, David Richter, James Romano, Elliot Rossen, Joyce Stanton, Mike Strauss, Karen Tates, Mary Jane Teeters-Eichacker, David Tilbor, Jonathan Weber, Mary Wheeler, Bob Wilhelm, Peggy Young, Sara Young, and Tyler Young.

Photo Credits
Cover: Robert Young and Ertl
Back Cover: Galoob
Ertl: Half-title page, 10, 33, 57; Robert Young: title page, 50, 58; Mattel: 6, 37; Galoob: 9, 11, 13, 28, 40, 44, 53; Brooklyn Museum: 16; Toy and Miniature Museum of Kansas City: 19; Detroit Children's Museum: 22, 23, 24, 25; Strombecker: 31; Everett Marshall III: 35; Matchbox: 47, 48; Brett Landrom: 55

Book design by Carol Matsuyama

Library of Congress Cataloging-in-Publication Data
Young, Robert, 1951-
    Miniature vehicles / by Robert Young. — 1st ed.
      p. cm. — (Collectibles)
    Includes index.
    Summary: Describes the history, popularity, and manufacture of various kinds of miniature vehicles and explains how to start a collection.
    ISBN 0-87518-518-5
    1. Vehicles—Models—Collectors and collecting—Juvenile literature. (1. Vehicles—Models.) I. Title. II. Series.
TL237.Y68   1993
629.22'1'075—dc20   92-33010

Dillon Press
Macmillan Publishing Company
866 Third Avenue
New York, NY 10022

Maxwell Macmillan Canada, Inc.
1200 Eglinton Avenue East
Suite 200
Don Mills, Ontario M3C 3N1

Macmillan Publishing Company is part of the Maxwell Communication Group of Companies.

First edition

Printed in the United States of America

10 9 8 7 6 5 4 3 2 1

CONTENTS

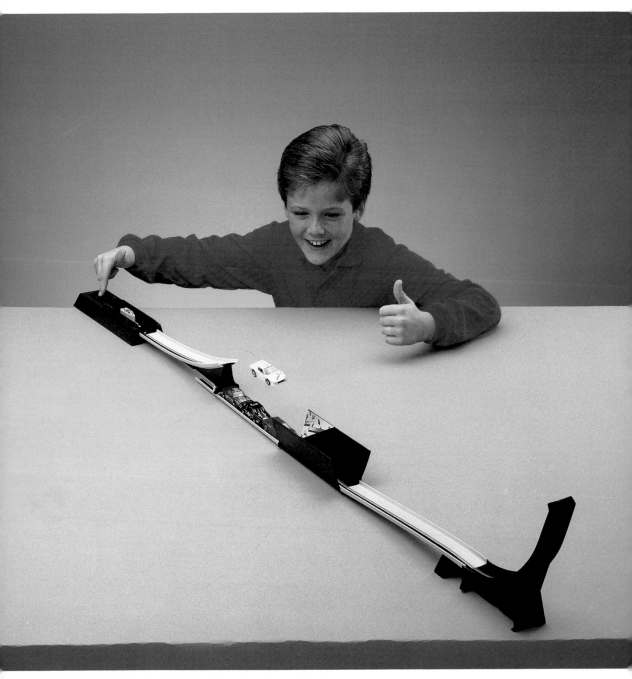

Whether you race them, jump them, or just display them, miniature vehicles are fun to play with.

CHAPTER 1

ALL KINDS OF VEHICLES

Your life would be a lot different without vehicles. Imagine what it would be like getting to school, going shopping, or taking a vacation. How would products made in other states or countries get to the stores in your community?

Luckily, we live in a world with many vehicles. You can't go very far without seeing a car, truck, motorcycle, bus, plane, or train. Vehicles make our lives a lot easier. They are also exciting and fun, which means people want to play with them and collect them—not exactly the vehicles themselves, but smaller versions of them. Small copies of vehicles are called miniature vehicles.

When you think of miniature vehicles, cars, trucks, boats, and planes probably come to your mind. But miniature vehicles were around long before these types of vehicles were ever invented. In 2500 B.C. children were playing with small vehicles made of baked clay. Since that time, children have played with toy versions of the popular vehicles of the day.

MINIATURE VEHICLES

These vehicles have been made of cardboard, many types of metal, plastic, rubber, and wood. Vehicles have even been made of a mixture of flour and glue. Today's miniature vehicles are mainly made of metal and plastic, or a combination of the two.

Miniature vehicles are very popular toys today. They are so popular that toy makers in the United States sell more than 100 million each year. And don't forget about the **accessories**.* These are the things that can be used with miniature vehicles, including carrying cases, play sets, and racetracks.

Why are these toys so popular? The reason is that people love cars, trains, horses and buggies— vehicles of all sorts. They also love toys and miniatures. And there are so many miniature vehicles from which to choose. Do you want a toy that looks like a real vehicle? If you do, you're in luck. There are toy makers that make their vehicles to scale. That means that everything about the toy is in correct proportion to the real vehicle, and often even the smallest details are copied.

Scale describes the relationship between the miniature vehicle and the full-size vehicle it is copying. The scale is shown by using fractions such as 1/8, 1/24, or 1/64. If a miniature vehicle is in 1/64 scale, that

*Words in **bold type** are explained in the glossary at the end of this book.

This can of "car wax" turns into a garage—one of the many accessories being made today.

means 64 of the miniature vehicles lined end to end would be the same length as the full-size vehicle. If the scale were 1/8, it would only take eight miniature vehicles to equal the full-size vehicle. So the larger the second number, the smaller the scale.

Scale miniature vehicles are divided into two main groups. Large-scale miniature vehicles include 1/43, 1/32, 1/24, 1/12, and 1/8 scales. Small-scale miniature vehicles include 1/64 and 1/128 scales. Because small-scale miniature vehicles are usually less expensive and easier to store, more of them are sold than large-scale.

Scale is just one of the many choices you have

These miniature tractors are in 1/64, 1/32, and 1/16 scale. The larger the second number in the fraction, the smaller the size of the miniature vehicle.

when it comes to miniature vehicles. You can choose from many different types, including farming, construction, and even space vehicles. There are miniature vehicles made in every color you can imagine, and there are even some without any color so that you can see inside them. You can buy miniature vehicles that go fast, talk, make sounds, light up, change colors, or transform into robots. With one line of vehicles, you create the design. And don't forget the vehicles that contain a secret world, or those that open up so that you can put smaller

There are so many different kinds of miniature vehicles. These are crystal clear, so you can see right through them.

vehicles inside them. There are even miniature vehicles that you can put money into.

It's not hard to find miniature vehicles to buy. They are sold in toy stores, hobby stores, and discount stores. You can buy them in person or through the mail. If you want used miniature vehicles, you can get them at flea markets or garage sales. If you want old miniature vehicles, try antique stores, collectors, or dealers (people who buy and sell them).

Miniature vehicles are fun and easy to collect. Since many are small, they can be stored and displayed easily. Compared with other collectibles, they don't cost very much, either. That's why thousands of kids around the world have become collectors.

Kids aren't the only ones who collect miniature vehicles. Adults collect them, too. For some adults, collecting is a good way to earn money. For others, collecting miniature vehicles helps them recall their childhoods.

For some people, collecting miniature vehicles leads to other things. In 1982 Mike Strauss of San Carlos, California, began collecting Hot Wheels. To build his collection, Strauss went to toy shows and auctions. He was surprised to find such a wide range of prices for the same model vehicles. It was hard to know whether the prices were fair. Strauss decided to do something about that.

Strauss talked to dealers and collectors to get information about the real value of the Hot Wheels vehicles. He averaged the prices these experts provided for each vehicle and published the results in a price guide. This gave collectors an idea of what a fair price was for the Hot Wheels.

Strauss published more price guides, as well as a newsletter for collectors. In 1989 Strauss formed the Hot Wheels Collectors Club to help Hot Wheels

These colorful models are made so that you can open them up and store smaller vehicles inside them.

collectors all over the world get together to share information and enjoyment of their hobby.

It took a lot of time to produce newsletters and start a worldwide club. But Mike Strauss still found time for the thing he loved: collecting miniature vehicles. By 1992, he had built up his collection to 20,000 vehicles!

You can have fun and learn a lot about collecting by joining clubs like the Hot Wheels Collectors Club. You can also read books and magazines, attend conventions, and visit museums.

MINIATURE VEHICLES

Museums in many parts of the world have miniature vehicles in their collections. There is even one museum that is totally made up of miniature vehicles.

The Matchbox Road Museum was started by Everett Marshall III in Newfield, New Jersey. Marshall had collected Matchbox vehicles as a kid, but left his hobby when he grew older. In 1980 Marshall began collecting again, and within ten years his house was filled with Matchbox vehicles. So he converted a three-car garage at his business site into a museum and opened it to the public in November of 1991. Since then many people have viewed his collection of nearly 13,000 miniature vehicles.

Wilbur Kohn, the postmaster of Dyersville, Iowa, didn't open his own museum to show his collection. Instead he loaned his 400 miniature trucks to a museum. His collection is viewed by thousands of people every year at the National Farm Toy Museum in Dyersville.

How did all this happen? How did miniature vehicles become so popular that people buy them, collect them, start clubs about them, and put them in museums? Let's start from the beginning. . . .

- Many miniature vehicles are **licensed**. That means the company that makes the real vehicle sells the rights, or gives a license, to others to produce them as toys.

- Sales of miniature vehicles and action figures are related. When people buy fewer action figures, sales of miniature vehicles go up.

- More than 20,000 people attend the Farm Toy Show held each year in Dyersville, Iowa.

- In 1989 more than $200 million worth of vehicle accessories were sold.

- An average of two Hot Wheels vehicles has been sold every second over the past 22 years. If all those vehicles were placed bumper to bumper, they would circle the earth more than two times.

- In 1990 London dealers Mint and Boxed sold a miniature wheeled fire-hose carrier for $1 million. Built in 1870 by George Brown and Company, this vehicle is made of tin and is hand-painted. It is the first toy ever to sell for a million dollars.

Children have been playing with miniature vehicles for thousands of years. This ram's head vehicle made of baked clay was used in Mesopotamia (present-day Iraq) some 4,500 years ago.

16

CHAPTER 2

MINIATURE VEHICLES THROUGH THE YEARS

It's not surprising that the first miniature vehicles looked a lot different from the miniature vehicles we have today. After all, there were no cars, trucks, planes, or trains hundreds of years ago.

The first miniature vehicles were simple toys with wheels. Around 2500 B.C. people called Sumerians lived in Mesopotamia, the land we know today as Iraq. The Sumerians made small, simple vehicles out of baked clay. They pulled these vehicles in ceremonies, and they may have used them as playthings, too.

Around 1200 B.C. Greek children were playing with horses and chariots made of baked clay. Some of these toys have been found in tombs, since it was a custom to bury children with their playthings. One reason for this custom was that the Greeks believed children would be able to play with the toys in the afterlife.

In 1100 B.C. craftspeople in Persia, present-day Iran, made animals that sat on platforms with wheels.

These animals, such as lions and porcupines, were carved from white limestone. A long string could be put through a small hole in the platform so that children could pull the animals around.

While these earliest examples were made of clay and limestone, wood has been the most popular material for making toys throughout history. Wood is light, easy to work, and hard to break. The problem is, wood decays over time. That's why it is hard to find old wooden vehicles. The oldest wooden toy around today that could even closely be considered a vehicle is a horse on wheels. It was made around 500 B.C. in Greece.

After that time children continued to play with simple, wheeled toys for several hundred years. Many of the toys were animals, but there were carts and wagons, too.

The Middle Ages in Europe was a time of castles and knights. Knights were soldiers who rode horses and served powerful lords. When knights weren't fighting, they trained hard. Part of their training was competing in tournaments.

There were many types of tournaments for knights, but the most common was made up of single combats, called **jousts**. In a joust, two knights on

For centuries wood was the most popular material used for making miniature vehicles. It was still being used in the 1850s, when this ride-on toy locomotive was built.

horseback would charge and try to knock each other off the horses, using long, blunt spears called **lances**.

Since jousts were so popular, toys were made of knights riding horses on wheels. Most were carved from wood, but some were made of metal, such as bronze. Children used string to pull the knights together and have their own jousts.

The 1500s brought changes for the craftspeople of Europe. Churches, which were once the major market for their products, were not buying as many things as they once had. As a result, craftspeople started making smaller objects for the home. Along with this change came another: People started collecting things.

Together, these changes helped bring about the toy industry. Because craftspeople were already organized, the toy industry was able to grow rapidly. For hundreds of years, craftspeople had belonged to guilds, which were similar to present-day unions.

Each special craft had its own guild. There was a guild for woodworkers, another guild for metalworkers, and still another for painters. While there was no guild for toy makers, members of each of these guilds made toys when time permitted. Guilds helped to keep the quality of products high and to protect the craftspeople from competition.

By the 1700s, Germany had become the most important toy-making area in the world. Germany had many skilled craftspeople living in its villages. It was also a land of dense forests, and the plentiful trees provided the wood from which to carve the toys.

From the villages, craftspeople took their finished toys to a central location. From there agents took toys and other finely carved wooden products to sell in markets all over the world. Because the town of Nuremberg was located close to so many toy makers, it became the center of the toy trade.

In 1740 a new material, called **composition**, was developed to make vehicles and other kinds of toys. A mixture of dark flour and glue, composition was easy to shape and could be poured into molds. While composition toys were easier to make than wooden toys, they never came close to being as popular.

The new material for making toys was only one of the many changes to come. The Industrial Revolution was about to change the world. Beginning in England in the mid 1700s, machines were invented that could produce goods faster than people working with their hands. It wasn't long before other countries—including France, Germany, and the United States—each had its own Industrial Revolution.

In France in 1815 a process was developed by which powerful presses stamped out toy parts from large sheets of tin. The parts were assembled by hand and the finished toy was boxed and then sold. Some of the tin for these toys came from people who recycled their food cans and other items made of the metal.

Soon toy factories began sprouting up all over Europe and the United States. These factories used tin and cast iron to **mass-produce** miniature vehicles, as well as other kinds of toys.

Then came the railroad. By 1830 railroads had been introduced in Europe as well as the United States and were changing the way people and goods were transported. Soon toy trains were being made. There were all kinds of toy trains. There were trains that had to be pushed along tracks, trains that were powered by steam, and trains that used springs to move. Some trains, called carpet-runners, came without tracks. By the late 1800s companies were making trains to scale. In 1884 the electric train was patented.

This early miniature train was called a carpet-runner. It came without tracks.

In the 1800s factories were turning out cast-iron toy vehicles of all kinds, like this brightly painted circus wagon.

In addition to trains, other vehicles of the day were developed into toys. These included circus wagons, fire trucks, and streetcars. Most, but not all, of the miniature vehicles made were based on full-size vehicles.

The Industrial Revolution continued throughout the 1800s. Soon new machines and processes

A 19th-century cast-iron fire engine

helped improve the toys being made. One improvement was the friction-drive system. It works when you roll the vehicle hard against your hand or along the floor. By doing this, you start a **flywheel** rotating inside the vehicle. The flywheel keeps the axle spinning, so when you set the vehicle down on the ground, it moves.

Another improvement was the introduction of **offset lithography**, a form of printing, in 1875. Before then, vehicles were sprayed or dipped into paint to color the large areas. Smaller details had to be hand-painted or done with the use of stencils. Offset lithography made it possible for machines to print color and details directly onto the metal. This helped save time and also made the vehicles look more re-alistic. Today special machines, which spray paint

One of the first train sets colored by using offset lithography, a form of printing introduced in the United States in 1875.

and apply decals, have replaced the use of offset lithography.

By 1900 toy making had become a major industry in the United States. American toys were being sent all over the world. Many of them were miniature vehicles, which had seen a great many changes in little more than a hundred years. But there were more changes to come.

FACTS TO COLLECT

- In 1608 a spring-powered toy coach was given to the future Louis XIII, seven-year-old son of the king of France.

- In Germany during the 1700s the system of using agents to sell toys was called publishing.

- Catalogs were first used to sell toys in the late 1770s in Europe.

- The years between 1840 and 1914 are known as the golden age of toys. That's because the toys of this period were so well crafted. Many combined machine-made parts with hand assembly and hand painting.

- Before the Civil War, most toys used by children in the United States were made in Europe.

Miniature vehicles have changed a lot since horse-and-buggy days. This snappy Micro Machine—in 1/128 scale—has been very popular since it was introduced in 1987.

CHAPTER 3

MODERN
MINIATURE VEHICLES

The early 1900s was a very exciting time. Many kinds of vehicles were being developed and improved in countries such as England, France, Germany, and the United States. As new vehicles were made and sold, toy copies of them soon followed. This helped many people get started in the business of making and selling miniature vehicles.

At this time most toy vehicles were cast in iron, shaped from tin, or carved out of wood. That changed in 1906, thanks to a company named Dowst Brothers and a simple item: the collar button.

The Dowst Brothers Company wasn't new in 1906. It began in 1876 as the publisher of the *National Laundry Journal*, a magazine for people in the laundry business. It also produced metal collar buttons. To make the collar buttons, a process called die-casting was used. Hot, molten metal was poured into a hollow mold in the shape of the button.

The success of the collar button led Dowst Brothers to begin die-casting other small items. The company made miniature irons, pans, and shoes and sold them to candy companies to be used as prizes.

In 1906 Dowst Brothers die-cast its first miniature vehicles. Over the next several years, more than 50 million of these toys were sold. The most popular was a copy of Henry Ford's famous Model T car. The toys were named Tootsietoys after Toots, a granddaughter of one of the Dowst brothers.

By the 1920s and 1930s a variety of miniature vehicles were being made by many different companies. Boats and planes and trains were being made. So were cars, trucks, motorcycles, farm vehicles, and construction equipment. Most of them were made of metal, and most were copies of real vehicles.

The popularity of miniature farm vehicles grew even more after Fred Ertl, Sr., was laid off in 1946. Ertl had been a molder for a company that made furnace parts in Dubuque, Iowa. Using his 23 years of experience, Ertl began making toy tractors in his home.

After buying scrap aluminum from a local company, Ertl melted the metal in his family furnace. He poured the molten metal into sand molds of tractors he had made. Ertl's family helped paint and assemble

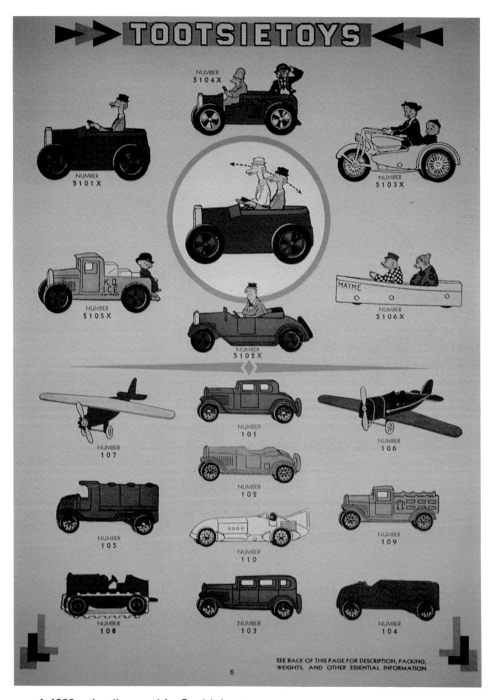

A 1933 advertisement for Tootsietoys

the tractors. Together, they could make as many as 150 tractors in a day.

People took notice of the well-made tractors the Ertl family produced. Sales were very good, and they got even better when the John Deere Company offered the Ertls a contract to make toy copies of its tractors. The Ertls used the money from that contract to help their business grow. Soon more contracts came in, and the Ertl Toy Company was on its way to becoming an important maker of miniature vehicles.

Other companies began making miniature vehicles around the same time. The Mound Metalcraft Company made its first toy vehicles, a steam shovel and a crane, in the basement of a small schoolhouse in Minneapolis, Minnesota. The company name was later changed to Tonka Toys after a local lake, Lake Minnetonka.

Another company, Nylint Corporation, had a hard time getting enough metal to make its toy cars and trucks. So Nylint bought scraps of steel from car makers in Detroit. Its miniature vehicles were made of the same materials used in real cars!

In 1947 two friends in England started a company that would make a lasting change in the toy-vehicle industry. Leslie Smith and Rodney Smith were not

A late-model Ertl tractor, one of the most popular miniature vehicles

related but were boyhood friends who were reunited in the British navy during World War II. When the war ended, the two men combined their money and their first names to form a company called Lesney Products.

With about $1,000 they bought a bombed-out tavern and some used die-cast machinery and began making metal parts for machines. When orders for their parts dropped, the two men started making toys. Their first attempt came in 1949 when they produced a road roller. Other types of toys followed, but vehicles sold the best.

Just as business began getting good for Lesney Products, the company was faced with a problem: It was not able to get zinc, a metal needed to make die-cast products. Because of the Korean War, the British government restricted the use of zinc to war-related items. From 1950 to 1952, Lesney made no die-cast toys. But that didn't keep the two men from planning.

In 1953, when toy companies could use zinc again, Lesney was ready with its plan. It would make vehicles, but they would be smaller and more affordable. Since it was the year Elizabeth II was to be crowned queen of England, Lesney decided to start by making a toy coronation coach, complete with horses pulling it. The coronation coach is the vehicle the queen rides in on the day she is crowned. More than a million of the five-inch toys were sold in 1953 alone!

Seeing how successful small vehicles were, Lesney decided to make more of them. The company made all kinds of vehicles, and it made them so small that each one could fit inside a matchbox. The idea of selling toys in matchboxes was so good that Lesney patented it so that no other company could do the same thing.

The Prime Mover, one of the first Matchbox vehicles

MINIATURE VEHICLES

It wasn't long before Matchbox vehicles became popular all over the world. For the next 15 years these miniatures set the standard for small-scale vehicles. Most were three inches long. They were inexpensive, made to last, and were so detailed that they even had treads on the tires.

Matchbox became the best-selling line of toy vehicles and may have continued to be, if it hadn't been for a man named Elliot Handler. Handler, one of the founders of Mattel Toys, was very interested in miniature vehicles. When he looked around to see what was being sold in 1967, he found that most vehicles had dull colors and wheels that didn't move very well.

Handler believed that children wanted more from their toys, that they wanted their vehicles to look better and go faster. He had the designers at Mattel work on a new kind of car. The car that they created had special sloped wheels that reduced friction. It also had thin axles made of piano wire. These were light and could turn very quickly. The car was fast, moving at a scale speed of 300 miles per hour downhill. When Handler saw the new car, he exclaimed, "Wow, those are hot wheels!" With that statement, the Hot Wheels line of miniature vehicles was born.

By 1987 Mattel was producing unusual-looking Hot Wheels, like this Zombat.

In addition to making the new cars fast, Mattel used racing designs and bright colors on its three-inch vehicles. In 1968, 16 different Hot Wheels models were sold for 59 cents each. They sold so well that nearly 16 million had to be made the first year!

Not to be outdone, Lesney designed a new line of miniature vehicles. These vehicles, called Superfast, were introduced in 1969. They had new types of wheels that allowed them to go faster than the older Matchbox vehicles.

Toy makers continued to look for new ways to improve their products—and their sales. One company took the idea of scale one step smaller. In 1987 Lewis Galoob Toys introduced Micro Machines,

MINIATURE VEHICLES

1¼-inch vehicles made in 1/128 scale. These tiny toys brought about a new, smaller category of car collecting. Within two years Micro Machines became the top-selling line of miniature vehicles.

Toy makers didn't change just the size of vehicles, The Universal Matchbox Group (which had bought out Lesney Products) and Mattel both introduced vehicles that changed color when put into water. These toys became such hits that in 1988, the first year of production, Mattel alone was making two million of its Color Racers every week.

Many more new and unusual miniature vehicles followed. Some were made to crash, light up, make sounds, or ride on air. More accessories became available. Large-scale miniature vehicles featured many details, like spare tires and hoods and trunks that open.

Changes will continue. There will always be new and exciting miniature vehicles being designed and sold. And this is very good news for collectors.

- Strombecker, started in 1876 as Dowst Brothers, is the oldest toy company still in business in the United States.

- The original design for packages of Matchbox vehicles came from a Scandinavian matchbox cover for Norvic Safety Matches.

- *Tonka* is a Sioux word meaning "great."

- In 1969 Mattel created a cartoon based on its Hot Wheels line of vehicles. The government stopped it from being shown, saying it was a "program-length commercial."

- Micro Machines may be small, but if all the ones sold in their first three years of production were stacked on top of one another, they would make a pile 5,958 miles tall.

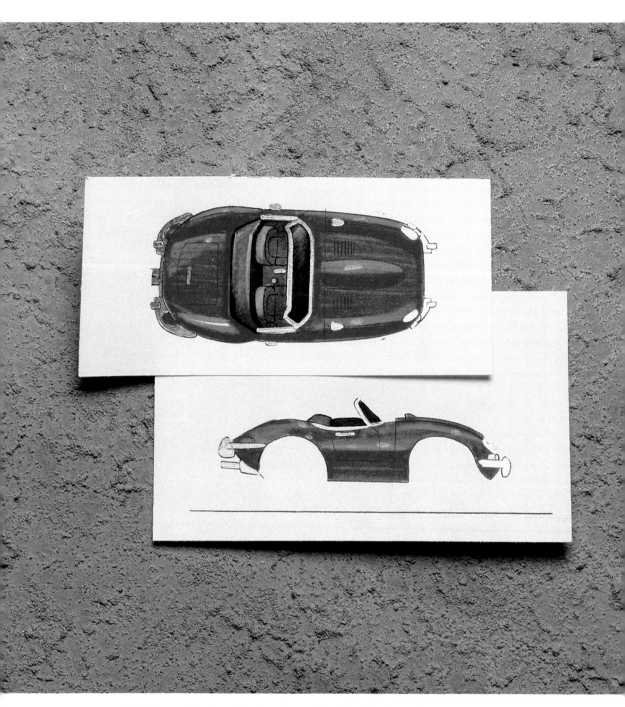

Miniature vehicles often begin on the drawing board.

CHAPTER 4

MAKING MINIATURE VEHICLES

Millions of miniature vehicles are produced every year. They are made by toy companies with the help of many different people, machines, and materials.

Like all products, miniature vehicles begin as ideas. Some ideas come from people who work for the company, like designers, engineers, or people in the licensing, marketing, or sales departments. Other ideas come from people outside the company, like collectors, inventors, or hobby-store owners.

To be considered, it helps if the idea can be shown to others. That is easy if the idea is based on vehicles that are made today. Photographs can be taken that show the inside, outside, and lots of real details. For ideas based on someone's imagination, drawings can be made.

Each toy company deals with ideas in its own way. In some companies, ideas for new products are considered by a small group of people called a review committee. Each member of the group represents a different department in the company, such as design, marketing, research and development, and sales.

The review committee members consider each idea. They want to choose toys that will fit in with their other products, and they want to make toys that many people will buy. To help them decide, the committee might have some market research done. That means having researchers show the drawings or photographs of the toy idea to children and parents to see if they would buy it.

If an idea based on a real vehicle is approved, the toy company must get permission from the manufacturer of the vehicle. That permission, called a licensing agreement, allows the toy company to make miniature copies of the vehicle. Often the toy company must agree to pay the manufacturer for its permission.

Now it is time for the idea to be developed. A designer makes more drawings of the vehicle. These drawings are sent to different departments of the company, which will each provide important information about the making of the vehicle.

The marketing department makes a sales forecast, an estimate of how many of these vehicles it thinks the company will be able to sell. The new product department figures what materials the vehicle will be made of and the cost of the molds. The engineering department makes a plan of how the vehicle will be put together and how much that will cost. The purchasing department comes up with the cost for buying the materials that will be used in making the vehicle.

After several months of work, each department sends its information back to the review committee. The review committee carefully considers the information before making the final decision of whether to add this vehicle to the company's toy line.

If the vehicle is approved, detailed drawings are made by engineers. Model makers use these drawings to make a **prototype**, or model, of the vehicle. Using sharp metal tools, the model makers carve the prototype out of Styrofoam or plastic. After it is painted, the prototype is used to help plan a schedule for production and to design packaging.

A master model of the body, the main part of the vehicle, is then carved out of plastic. It is made larger than the miniature vehicle will be so that even the smallest details can be shown. Model makers then place the master model inside a wooden frame and pour liquid plastic around it. When the

A prototype carved from plastic—one of the first steps in making a miniature vehicle.

plastic dries, the model is removed, leaving a cast in the shape of a vehicle. This is called a cavity cast.

Model makers press a thin layer of beeswax into the cavity cast and then pour liquid plastic into it. When the plastic dries, workers remove it. This part becomes the core cast. The wax is taken out of the cavity cast so that there will be space between these two parts when they are made into molds. That space will be filled with liquid metal and become the body of the miniature vehicle.

The cavity cast and the core cast, called tooling aids, are then made into production molds. Production molds are made of metal so that they will last a long time without cracking or breaking. To make the molds, toolmakers use a special machine called a **panagraph**. On one side of the machine, a small tip moves around the tooling aids and measures them. Information about the size and shape of the aids is relayed to another part of the machine that automatically cuts the exact same shapes—but in a smaller size—into a block of hard steel.

When the molds are completed, several are put into a holding block that is bolted into a die-casting machine. Production of miniature vehicles can begin.

Workers put 40-pound bars of zinc, called **ingots**, into a large tank at the end of the die-casting machine. When the ingots are heated to 800°F, they melt into a liquid. The die-casting machine pumps the hot metal out of the tank and squirts it into the holding block, filling each of the molds.

Within five seconds, the metal has cooled and become solid. The holding block automatically opens, and small pins push the metal pieces out of the molds. The pieces of metal are in the shape of vehicles, but they are connected to one another by thin pieces of metal. A worker uses a large pair of pliers to reach in and pull the parts from the machine. The parts are then put onto a conveyor belt.

The conveyor belt takes the metal parts to a machine called a trim press. The trim press separates the vehicle bodies by pushing them apart. The extra metal that connected the bodies is put into a chute that returns it to the hot tank of liquid metal. There it can be remelted and used again.

Not all the excess metal has been removed from the bodies. There are still small, sharp pieces of extra metal called **burrs,** or flashing. These pieces must be removed so that the vehicles will be safe to handle. Sometimes workers remove the burrs. Other times vehicle parts are dumped into a large barrel and tumbled for five minutes. As the parts bang together, they knock the burrs off one another.

The deburred parts are put onto another conveyor and sent through a machine that washes, rinses, and dries them. The parts are inspected, put into containers, and taken to the painting area.

At the painting area, workers hang the parts on hooks attached to tall metal frames. After a motor has moved the frames into a booth, a painting machine sprays the parts with paint. When the paint has dried, workers take the parts off the hooks and put them into boxes. If the vehicles need decals, the parts are put onto a conveyor belt that carries them past a special machine. This machine uses soft, spongelike pads to push on decals. The parts are

A worker removes the burrs from miniature vehicle parts.

now ready to be **assembled**, or put together.

Miniature vehicles can be assembled by machines or by workers and machines. In companies where workers are used, the metal bodies of the vehicles are put into boxes and delivered to workers operating assembling machines. Parts made in other factories, such as the wheels and axles and the plastic bottoms and insides of the vehicles, are also taken to the workers.

Workers pull a drawerlike piece out of the machine and place the metal body into it upside down. The plastic parts, along with the wheels and axles, are positioned on the body. The worker slides the

Parts are spray-painted by machine. Later, decals are added and the parts are assembled.

"drawer" into the machine and presses a button. In a few seconds the machine has snapped the pieces together, using high pressure.

The worker then pulls the assembled vehicle from the machine, inspects it, and puts it into a container. When the container is filled, the completed toys are taken to be packaged and then boxed.

The miniature vehicles are ready to be shipped to stores all over the world for people of all ages to buy and enjoy.

- Most miniature vehicles are made in the Far East.

- In 1959 Mattel became the first toy company to use market research.

- From idea to finished product, it takes about 16 months to produce a new miniature vehicle.

- Making molds for a miniature vehicle can cost more than $200,000.

- The Fashion Institute of Technology in New York City offers a college degree program in toy design.

- Mattel has produced more than one billion Hot Wheels vehicles, using more than 50,000 tons of metal.

You can learn a lot about collecting by visiting a miniature vehicle museum.

CHAPTER 5

COLLECTING MINIATURE VEHICLES

Now that you know about miniature vehicles, how would you like to collect them? Collecting miniature vehicles can be an enjoyable hobby.

To start, think about why you want to collect vehicles. Is it because you like to look at them or play with them? Or maybe you want to make money. Your reason for collecting will be important in deciding what vehicles to add to your collection.

There are many, many ways to set up a miniature vehicle collection. Some people start with the vehicles they already have and build from there. Others start with no vehicles and carefully choose each addition to their collection.

Since there are so many miniature vehicles around, collectors often decide to limit their collections. Some only collect vehicles made during a certain time period, from a specific manufacturer, or from a particular country. Others limit their collections to vehicles made of a certain material, such as cast iron, plastic, rubber, steel, or tin. Still others choose to collect only vehicles of one scale, such as 1/64 or 1/16. And then there are many collectors who focus their collections on vehicles of the same type, such as cars, farm vehicles, fire engines, or space vehicles.

Don't feel you have to be limited by the way other people collect. Make up your own plans for collecting. That's what makes collecting fun.

Once you decide what you want to collect, it's time to start finding vehicles. The first place to look is right around you. You might be surprised at what you can find without leaving your own home. Search through your closet, look in your drawers, explore your attic, cellar, and any other place toys are kept or stored.

Once you've searched your home, talk to your relatives. Tell them you are starting a miniatuie vehicle collection and let them know what kinds of vehicles you are looking for. Grandparents, aunts, uncles, and cousins can be great resources for collectors.

At some point you will probably want to buy some vehicles for your collection. That's easy if you are collecting vehicles that are still being made. All you have to do is go to a toy, hobby, department, or discount store and buy them. If you want to save

Some people collect only vehicles made to a certain scale, like these Micro Machines.

money, you can find used vehicles at flea markets or garage sales.

Collecting older vehicles is a bit more challenging. You will find it easier to buy them if you know something about them. So how do you find out about older vehicles? You read, you look, you ask questions, and you listen. Go to your library and ask for books on toy collecting. See if they have any collecting magazines. If the library doesn't have any of the books or magazines you are looking for, try a toy, hobby, or book store. Reading about older vehicles will not only help you identify them, but will also help you learn how much they are worth.

Learn all you can about miniature vehicles. Visit museums that have vehicles in their collections, attend toy shows and conventions, and join collecting clubs. Don't forget to talk to people, too. Talk to dealers as well as to other collectors.

Once you know about older vehicles, try finding some to buy. Look in antique stores and second-hand stores. Try auctions, estate sales, toy shows, and conventions. You can also find vehicles for sale in the classified ads of toy and collecting magazines and in collecting-club newsletters.

Once you have a collection of vehicles, what are you going to do with them? For one thing, you can play with them. Create a world of your own and use your vehicles to help the people work, play, and transport themselves from place to place.

Maybe you want to race your vehicles. You can start with something simple like taking a cushion from your couch and putting it at an angle so that

Brett and Clinton Landrom of Vinita, Oklahoma, have limited their collection to tractors—hundreds of them!

your vehicles will roll down it. If you get serious about racing, you can buy tracks on which to race small-scale vehicles. Or you can make your own out of wood.

Buy a sheet of plywood and some thin strips of wood. Nail the strips to the plywood to make lanes for the cars. Leave some space at the end where you want the vehicles to start. That way you can hold a piece of wood across the track to line up the cars and then lift it to start the race. Elevate one end of the plywood, line up your vehicles at the starting line, and go!

Another thing you can do with your vehicles is display them. You can display miniature vehicles almost anywhere. Line them up on a windowsill, arrange them on a shelf, put them on your desk.

Use your imagination to display your vehicles. Buy or make a display case. You can create a scene with your vehicles in a cardboard box, for example. Or you can use a plastic soda bottle to make a diorama. First, dip the bottom half of the bottle into hot water. This will soften the glue used to connect the two bottle parts. When the glue is soft, pull the two pieces apart. Lay the bottle on its side and create a scene inside it using your

If you like sports cars, you can collect many different types. The doors and hood open on this sleek red Ferrari.

It's fun to create a scene with your miniature vehicles.

vehicles and other materials, such as miniature shrub-bery, rocks, and dirt. When you are finished, carefully push the bottom of the bottle back into place. Cut cardboard or wood to make a support for your diorama.

As a collector, you will want to take good care of your miniature vehicles. Taking care of vehicles is easy. To keep them clean, about all you have to do is wipe them off with a cloth. Avoid leaving your vehicles in direct sunlight for long periods of time because the paint will fade. To prevent rust, keep your vehicles in a dry area. It's also a good idea to use a carrying case when you want to take your vehicles from place to place. Be careful about play-ing with them, too. Rough play can chip the paint off your vehicles or break or dent them.

What should you do if any of your vehicles need repair? Well, that depends. If it's something simple like replacing a tire, you could probably do it your-self. Get the parts at a hobby store or at a toy show. For more difficult repairs, check with a dealer or other collector to find someone who fixes toys. Always get an estimate of how much it's going to cost before allowing the repairs to be done. But beware—repairing or repainting an older vehicle can often lower its value.

Someday you might want to sell some of the vehicles in your collection. If you have modern vehicles, try selling them at a garage sale or flea market. Base your selling price on the condition of your vehicles and on whether they are still being made and how much people want them.

For older vehicles, do some research before deciding on a price. Check collecting books and magazines. Talk to dealers and other collectors. When you have decided on a fair price, let local dealers and collectors know what your price is. Place an ad in your local paper or in a collecting magazine.

There is a lot to learn by having a miniature vehicle collection. You can make some money, too. Best of all, you can have fun by collecting miniature vehicles!

FACTS TO COLLECT

- In 1991 people spent more money on Galoob's Micro Machines than on any other brand of miniature vehicle.

- Vehicles that were originally sold as part of a set often become more valuable than vehicles that were sold separately.

- Vehicles that have been repainted are worth half as much as those with their original paint.

- More than nine million boys collect Hot Wheels vehicles. Each owns an average of 24 cars.

- The average number of vehicles owned by an adult Hot Wheels collector is 1,420.

- The most valuable Hot Wheels vehicle is the 1974 Road King dump truck, which is worth more than $600.

- The 1947 soapbox racer made by Lesney can sell for more than $2,000. Only 12 of these vehicles are known to exist.

MINIATURE VEHICLE TIME LINE

2500 B.C. —Sumerians make miniature vehicles of baked clay.

1200 B.C. —Greek children play with wheeled horses and chariots made of baked clay.

1100 B.C. —Persian craftspeople make wheeled animal toys.

500 B.C. —Greeks make wheeled toys out of wood.

1200s —Children in Europe play with miniature knights on wheels.

1500s —The toy-making industry begins in Europe.

1700s —Germany is the leading toy maker in the world.

1740 —Composition is used to make miniature vehicles.

1815 —Machines are first used to make toys in France; toy factories begin to mass-produce.

1830	—Railroads are popular in several countries; toy trains are made soon after.
late 1800s	—Miniature versions are made of the popular vehicles of the day.
1890s	—Offset lithography is used to paint miniature vehicles, making them look realistic.
1906	—Dowst Brothers die-casts its first miniature vehicles, which later are named Tootsietoys.
1920s and 1930s	—Many companies are making a variety of miniature vehicles.
1946	—Fred Ertl, Sr., begins making toy tractors in his home.
1949	—Lesney Products begins making the die-cast vehicles that will later be called Matchbox toys.
1968	—Mattel makes its first Hot Wheels vehicles; 16 million are sold in the first year.
1969	—Matchbox creates its Superfast line of vehicles to compete with Hot Wheels.

1987 —Lewis Galoob Toys introduces Micro Machines, 1/128 scale vehicles.

1988 —Universal Matchbox and Mattel both come out with miniature vehicles that change color.

1990 —A hand-painted fire-hose carrier made in 1870 is sold for $1 million by dealers Mint and Boxed of London.

1991 —The Matchbox Road Museum is opened in Newfield, New Jersey.

FOR MORE INFORMATION

For more information about toys, write to:

> Communications Department
> Toy Manufacturers of America
> 200 Fifth Ave.
> New York, NY 10010
> (toy fact booklet, "Betcha Didn't Know")

For more information about careers in toy making, write to:

> Judy Ellis, Chairperson
> Toy Design Department
> Fashion Institute of Technology
> Seventh Ave. and 27th St.
> New York, NY 10001

For more information about miniature vehicles and particular brands, contact:

> The Ertl Company
> P.O. Box 500
> Dyersville, IA 52040
>
> Matchbox Toys
> 141 W. Commercial Ave.
> Moonachie, NJ 07074
>
> Mattel Toys
> (800) 421-2887

Spec-Cast
P.O. Box 324
Dyersville, IA 52040

For more information about miniature vehicles in magazines, write to:

Antique Toy World
P.O. Box 34509
Chicago, IL 60634

Cruising Connection
2648 E. Workman Ave., Suite 413
West Covina, CA 91791

Spec-tacular News
Box 324
Dyersville, IA 52040

Toy Farmer
HC 2 Box 5, Dept. TT
LaMoure, ND 58458

Toy Trucker & Contractor
HC 2 Box 5, Dept. BB
LaMoure, ND 58458

For more information about miniature vehicle clubs, write to:

American International Matchbox, Inc.
532 Chestnut St.
Lynn, MA 01904

The Ertl Collectors' Club
P.O. Box 500
Dyersville, IA 52040

Hot Wheels Collectors Club
26 Madera Ave.
San Carlos, CA 94070

Matchbox Collectors Club
P.O. Box 278
Durham, CT 06422

Places to visit:

Chester Toy Museum
13a Lower Bridge Street
Chester
Cheshire, England

Children's Museum
Detroit Public School
67 East Kirby
Detroit, MI 48202

The Children's Museum of Indianapolis
3000 North Meridian Street
Indianapolis, IN 46206

Detroit Antique Toy Museum
6325 West Jefferson
Detroit, MI 48209

Essex Institute
132 Essex Street
Salem, MA 01970

Henry Ford Museum & Greenfield Village
P.O. Box 1970
Dearborn, MI 48121

Matchbox Road Museum
17 Pearl Street
Newfield, NJ 08344

Nashville Toy Museum
2613B McGavock Pike
Nashville, TN 37214

National Farm Toy Museum
1110 16th Ave., SE
Dyersville, IA 52040

Please Touch Museum
210 North 21st Street
Philadelphia, PA 19103

The Toy and Miniature Museum of Kansas City
5235 Oak Street
Kansas City, MO 64112

GLOSSARY

accessories (ik-SES-uh-reez)—items such as carrying cases, play sets, and racetracks that can be used with miniature vehicles

assemble—to put together

burr—a small, sharp piece of extra metal on miniature vehicles

composition (komp-uh-ZI-shun)—a mixture of flour and glue, once used to make miniature vehicles

flywheel—a heavy wheel attached to a vehicle that regulates its speed

ingot (ING-gut)—a bar of metal

joust (jowst)—combat between two knights on horseback in the Middle Ages; each knight was armed with a lance and wore armor

lance—a long, pointed spear

license (LI-sens)—permission to produce a product

mass-produce—to make many at one time

offset lithography (OFF-set) (lih-THOG-ruh-fee)—a process of printing onto a surface such as paper or metal

panagraph (PAN-uh-graff)—a machine used to make production molds; it makes exact copies of miniature vehicle casts

prototype (PROHT-uh-type)—the first model of a new product

scale—the size of a miniature vehicle compared with the real-life vehicle

INDEX

ABOUT THE AUTHOR

A fourth-grade teacher and free-lance writer, Robert Young is fascinated by kids and the things they collect. In addition to the books in the Collectibles series, Mr. Young has written about a wide range of subjects. *The Chewing Gum Book* and *Sneakers: The Shoes We Choose!* are two of his titles recently published under the Dillon Press imprint. Mr. Young lives with his family in Eugene, Oregon, and enjoys visiting schools and talking to teachers and students about writing.